Homes

Written by Sally Hewitt

W

FRANKLIN WATTS

LONDON•SYDNEY

First published in 2009 as *Starting Geography: Homes*
by Franklin Watts
This edition 2013

338 Euston Road, London NW1 3BH

Franklin Watts Australia
Level 17/207 Kent Street, Sydney NSW 2000

Copyright © Franklin Watts 2009

Editor: Katie Dicker
Art Direction: Dibakar Acharjee (Q2AMedia)
Designer: Ritu Chopra (Q2AMedia)
Picture researcher: Kamal Kumar (Q2AMedia)
Craft models made by: Shweta Nigam (Q2AMedia)
Photography: Tarang Saggar (Q2AMedia)

Picture credits:
t=top b=bottom c=centre l=left r=right

Cover: Frank Chmura/Age Fotostock/Photolibrary
Title page: Jacques Kloppers/Shutterstock
Insides: Dhoxax/Shutterstock: 6l, Jacques
Kloppers/Shutterstock: 6r, Michael Boys/Corbis: 7tr,
FloridaStock/Shutterstock: 7b, Nne Van Der
Wal/Corbis: 8, Wojtek Buss/Age
Fotostock/Photolibrary: 9tr, Rachel
Dewis/Istockphoto: 9cr, Lillis
Photography/Istockphoto: 9bl, Gorin/Shutterstock:
9br, Denise Kappa/Shutterstock: 10, BL Images
Ltd/Alamy: 11tr, Vera Bogaerts/Shutterstock: 12tr,
Mastering_Microstock/Shutterstock: 12bl, Jeffrey
Banke/123rf: 14, Andrew Holt/Alamy:15tr,
CreatOR76/Shutterstock: 15br, Elizabeth Whiting &
Associates/Alamy: 16cr, Jorge Salcedo/Shutterstock:
16b, Slobodan/Shutterstock: 17tr, Patricia
Hofmeester/Shutterstock: 18, Dainis
Derics/Shutterstock: 19tr, Photofusion Picture
Library/Alamy: 20, Picture Contact/Alamy: 21tr,
Historical Picture Archive/Corbis: 22cl, Jordan
Rooney/Alamy: 22br, Andrew Butterton/Alamy: 24,
Paul Glendell/Alamy: 25, Julia Waterlow; Eye
Ubiquitous/Corbis: 26cl, Klaus Mellenthin/
Jupiter images: 26br, Peter Adams/Image Bank/Getty
Images: 27.
Q2AMedia Image Bank: Imprint page, Contents page,
19, 21, 23.
Q2AMedia Art Bank: 11, 13, 17, 27.

With thanks to our models Shruti Aggarwal,
Jyotsna Julka.

Every attempt has been made to clear copyright.
Should there be any inadvertent omission, please
apply to the publisher for rectification.

A CIP catalogue record for this book
is available from the British Library

ISBN: 978 1 4451 1922 9

Dewey Classification: 728

Printed in China

Franklin Watts is a division of Hachette Children's
Books, an Hachette UK company.
www.hachette.co.uk

Contents

Words that appear in **bold** can be found in the glossary on pages 28–29.

What are homes?

Homes are where we live. Around the world you can see homes of different shapes and sizes. The first homes were very simple with one room and a fire for cooking and keeping warm.

People around the world live in very different homes – from large brick buildings to small mud huts.

Cities and villages

Our homes can be found in cities, towns or villages. In the city, many homes are crowded together in rows of houses or blocks of **flats**. In villages, homes usually have more space around them.

Inside and outside

The inside and outside of a home can look different from place to place. The design of a home will depend on where you live, what the weather is like and what the local building **traditions** are.

■ This traditional Moroccan home has wooden shutters and painted tiles. They decorate the home and keep it cool.

Home detectives

Homes can tell us a lot about a place. Old buildings are usually made of **materials** that were found locally long ago. Large houses built with expensive materials are the homes of rich people. Homes that are crowded together often show an area where lots of workers live.

■ This large house is the home of a rich family. It was built with expensive materials and is in beautiful surroundings.

Settlements

Long ago, people chose a place to build a **settlement** carefully. A hill was good for defence against attack, a valley provided **shelter** from the weather and a **fertile plain** was good for growing crops.

By the water

Big cities, such as London, New York and Sydney, grew from settlements built around the mouth of a great river. Ships brought in people and **trade** from overseas. The river carried people and goods inland.

New York City grew when people travelled to the USA by boat to begin a new life.

Growing settlements

Settlements grow bigger over time. Towns and cities usually begin as a few houses clustered together. Over the years, newer houses are built around the edges as more people move to the area. In contrast, in a modern **new town**, the homes are all built within a few years of each other.

Old and newer houses stand next to each other in a city that has been growing for hundreds of years.

Find out the history of your area

1 With an adult, take photos or draw sketches of the different styles of homes near to where you live.

2 Can you find out when they were built?

3 Which is the oldest home you can find? Which is the newest?

How old is your home?

My house – 1999

A new block of flats

Oldest house – 1820

9

Locality

Your **locality** is the area where you live. It might be the countryside, the seaside, a busy city or a housing estate. Going for a walk around your neighbourhood will tell you about your locality.

City or suburbs

In the city, many people live in flats. They don't have a car, so they walk or take the train or bus to work. **Suburbs** are the areas around the edges of a city. People who live in the suburbs often have further to travel to work or to the shops.

A suburban house usually has a garage. The family may use the car to drive to work, school or the shops.

In a village

Homes in the centre of a village can be very old. They have often been there for hundreds of years. Newer homes are built around the edges of a village.

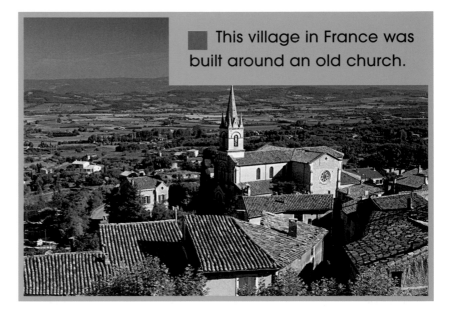
This village in France was built around an old church.

Find out about your locality

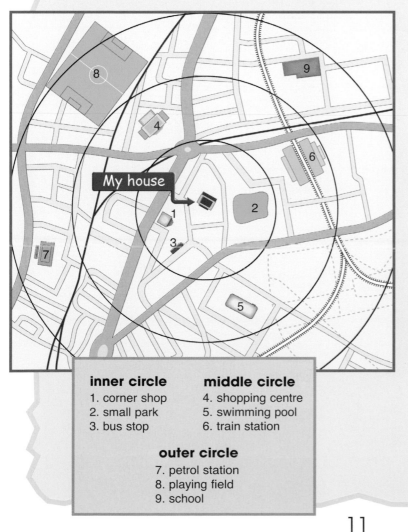

My house

inner circle
1. corner shop
2. small park
3. bus stop

middle circle
4. shopping centre
5. swimming pool
6. train station

outer circle
7. petrol station
8. playing field
9. school

1 Print a copy of a map of where you live from the Internet with your home in the centre of the map.

2 Mark your home. Draw a small circle with your home in the centre.

3 Now draw two more circles each larger than the one before.

Write a list of everything that you can see within each circle.

Designing buildings

Homes around the world have many different designs. They are often built with local materials and designed to suit the landscape and **climate** of an area.

Shelter

Homes are built to shelter us from the weather. Where there is lots of rain and snow, homes have sloping roofs. In areas that flood, houses are built on stilts to keep them above the water. In hot countries, thick walls and small windows keep out the heat.

This house in Thailand has stilts to keep it above the water.

Traditional Japanese houses have wooden frames and paper walls.

Earthquakes

Homes built in earthquake zones, such as Japan, are in danger of falling down during an earthquake. They are designed and built to move, but not collapse, if the ground shakes.

Match the homes

You will need:

- card • scissors
- pencils and pens

1 Draw your own pictures of these children and homes onto playing-card sized rectangles.

I live in a hot, dry place

I live where we have earthquakes

3 Take it in turns to pick a card. Turn the card over to show your friends. Then pick another card. Have you matched a child with their home? If yes, take the cards. If not, replace them. The winner is the person with the most 'matched' cards.

2 Shuffle the cards and put them face down on the floor.

I live where it often floods

4 Add to the game by finding some more children and their homes.

I live in a cold, snowy place

Home materials

Homes all over the world are made from lots of different materials – from reeds and mud to concrete and steel. What is your home made from?

Local materials

People traditionally used to build their homes from materials found nearby. Local rock makes a strong, long-lasting material. Trees provide wood for log cabins in forests and reeds are used to build homes near a lake.

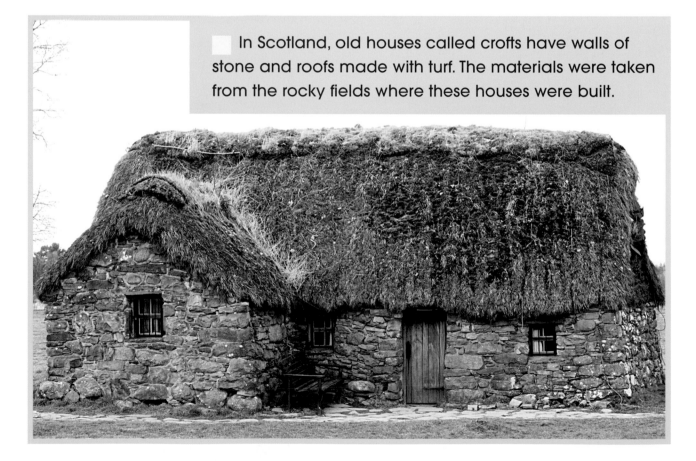

In Scotland, old houses called crofts have walls of stone and roofs made with turf. The materials were taken from the rocky fields where these houses were built.

Modern materials

Modern homes are built from **manufactured** materials, such as concrete, glass, metal and plastic. These strong, long-lasting materials are often cheap to make and can be easily transported to different areas.

This tall, strong building is made from steel and glass. It has good views from the big windows.

Do a survey of the materials used to build your home

Make a chart like the one below to record the materials used to build your home both inside and outside.

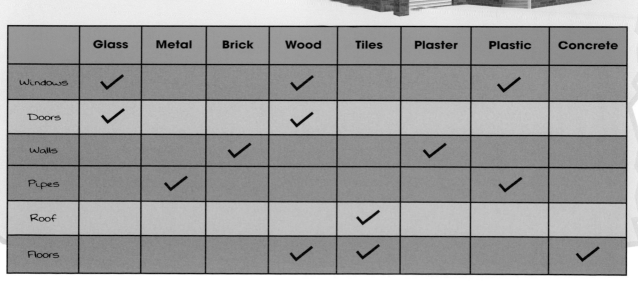

	Glass	Metal	Brick	Wood	Tiles	Plaster	Plastic	Concrete
Windows	✓			✓			✓	
Doors	✓			✓				
Walls			✓			✓		
Pipes		✓					✓	
Roof					✓			
Floors				✓	✓			✓

15

Inside

Homes keep us safe and give us shelter. A home is somewhere to spend time and to sleep. Homes are also a place to store our belongings.

Different rooms

Inside our homes, we divide the space into rooms or areas for the different things we do. Bedrooms are for sleeping, the kitchen for cooking, the bathroom for washing and the living room for relaxing.

■ George helped to choose the colours to decorate his bedroom. This room is full of his books and toys.

■ This big open-plan area is designed for cooking, eating and relaxing.

Floor plan

A floor plan is a drawing that clearly shows the layout of the inside of a home. It is an **aerial view** looking down on the rooms from above. It gives important information about the size and number of rooms.

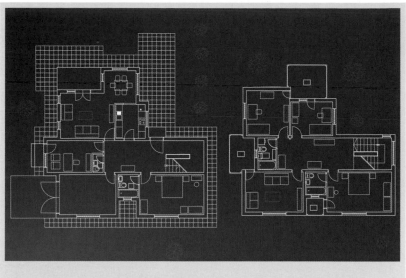

This is a floor plan of a house with two floors.

Design a house

1 Draw a floor plan of a house you would like to live in.

2 Think about who will live with you. What will you all need? How many floors will there be? How many rooms? Will there be a garden?

3 First, draw the ground floor. Any floors you add will need to fit on top. You can choose the number and size of the rooms on each floor.

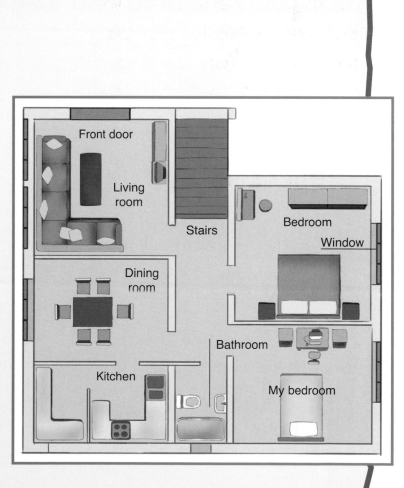

Big homes

Sometimes, rulers and rich people build palaces, villas and mansions to show off their power and wealth. These huge houses are built with expensive materials, such as marble, and are protected by high walls.

Tourist attractions

Some grand historic homes are open for you to visit. You can look at these impressive buildings, learn about their history, see paintings and other treasures and enjoy the beautiful gardens.

The people of the USA built the White House as a home for their president.

Fairytale castle

About 150 years ago, King Ludwig II of Bavaria (in Germany) built Neuschwanstein Castle for his home. Walt Disney modelled Sleeping Beauty's palace on the outline that Neuschwanstein Castle makes against the sky.

Neuschwanstein Castle was built high on a hill.

Make a silhouette of a house on a hill

You will need:
• paper – black and blue
• pencil • scissors • glue

1 On the black paper, copy in pencil the shape of the castle in the picture above (or use your imagination to draw your own castle, palace or mansion).

2 Cut out the shape of your building and the shape of a hill.

3 Stick the shapes onto the blue paper to make a silhouette of a house on a hill.

Small homes

Small homes can be useful in areas where there is not much space. Because land and buildings are very expensive, small homes are also cheaper to buy.

Industry and farms

Small cottages on farmland were traditionally homes for farm workers. In towns and cities, rows of small houses were built quickly and cheaply for workers in factories, mills and mines.

These houses were built close together. Each house shares side walls with its neighbours.

One room

In some of the poorest parts of the world, large families live together and sleep, eat and cook in just one room. After a war or a natural disaster, such as an earthquake, survivors live in crowded temporary camps or shelters.

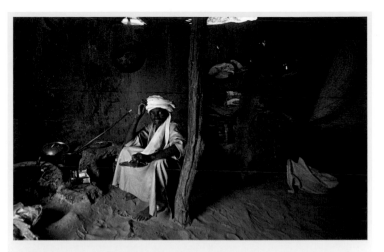

This African boy is cooking over a fire. The room is also his family's bedroom.

Make a model one-room house

You will need:
- 2 card circles the same size (draw around a side plate)
- scissors • brown and yellow paint • self-hardening clay
- art straws • glue

1 Fold one circle into quarters and cut out a segment. Fold the circle round and glue the sides together to make a cone for the roof. Cut a hole at the top for the chimney.

2 Paint the other circle brown. Draw a smaller circle in the middle for the house to stand on.

3 Mould brick shapes from self-hardening clay and build your house in a cylinder shape on the card, leaving a space for the entrance.

4 Paint the art straws yellow. Stick them all around the cone and trim them to make a thatched roof.

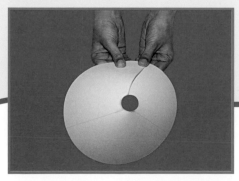

Mobile homes

Nomadic people move with their animals looking for land, food and water. Some carry their homes with them. Others build shelters and leave them behind when they move on.

The plains people of North America followed buffalo herds. They dragged a tent, called a tepee, along on a sledge.

Travelling around

In Europe, travellers used to move from place to place looking for work. They lived in decorated caravans pulled by a horse. Today, caravans are often used as mobile holiday homes. People travel from place to place with everything they need for sleeping, washing and cooking.

This traditional caravan was used by European travellers.

Make a model caravan

You will need:
- thin card • cardboard
- shoebox • scissors • hole punch • glue • paint and coloured pens • 2 straws
- poster putty or sticky tape

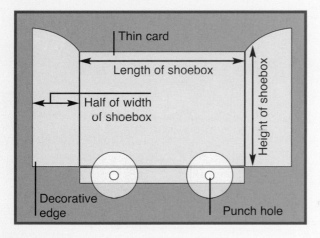

Thin card

Length of shoebox

Half of width of shoebox

Height of shoebox

Decorative edge

Punch hole

1 Cut the card, as shown above, to make one side of the caravan. Repeat for the other side. Punch holes for the wheel axles to go through. Stick the card to the shoebox to make the body of the caravan.

2 Cut a rectangle of card slightly bigger than the shoebox base and glue it onto the body for a curved roof. Cut four cardboard circles for the wheels and punch a hole in their centre.

3 Use bright paints (including gold and silver) or coloured pens to decorate the parts of your caravan. Use the picture on page 22 for ideas.

4 Push the straws through the axle holes and fix the wheels to the end of the straws with poster putty or sticky tape.

23

Eco-homes

Many new homes are **eco-homes**. These are designed to be as kind to the **environment** as possible. Older homes can be adapted to be more eco-friendly. A simple draught excluder, for example, can stop heat escaping and save **energy**.

wind turbine

solar panel

Renewable energy

Eco-homes use renewable energy for heating and lighting. Renewable energy comes from sources such as sunlight, water and wind that will never run out. In most homes, **fossil fuels** are burned for energy. These fuels give out **carbon emissions** that harm the environment, and will eventually run out.

This eco-home has solar panels to heat water and wind turbines to generate electricity.

Make a difference

There are lots of things that can be done to make your home more environmentally friendly. **Double-glazing** the windows to keep out draughts, using **insulation** to keep in the heat, mending dripping taps and re-using bath water are just a few examples.

Loft insulation keeps a house warm and cosy. It helps to reduce heating bills, too!

How eco-friendly is your home?

1 Carry out a survey like the one shown below.

2 Tick the boxes and find out if your home is an eco-home.

3 Ask your family what changes you could make to improve things.

SAVE ENERGY	Double-glazing	Draught excluders	Stand-by off (TV, computer, etc.)
	✓	Make!	✓
SAVE WATER	Mend dripping taps	Use shower instead of bath	Collect rainwater
	✓	✓	Research!
PLANTS	Wild area in garden	Green leafy plants	Window boxes
	✓	✓	Make!

Unusual homes

All over the world, people live in unusual homes that probably look very different to your own home. In northern China, people carve homes out of the mountainside. They are easy and cheap to build!

■ These cave homes in China look very basic, but they have electricity and running water.

Ice and snow

Inuit people of the frozen Arctic traditionally build shelters called igloos. Blocks of packed snow provide shelter when the Inuit people are out on hunting and fishing trips.

■ This igloo is warm because snow keeps out the cold and keeps in the heat.

Reed islands

By Lake Titicaca in Peru, local people weave the reeds that grow around the lake into floating islands, shelters and boats. The women constantly repair and replace the reeds that rot in the water.

These shelters by Lake Titicaca are made using local reeds.

A day in the life...

Imagine what it would be like to live in any of the three homes described here.

Write about a day in your life, living in one of them.

Today, I woke to the sound of feet crunching on snow...

Today, I woke to the sound of splashing water...

Today, I woke to the sound of birds flying to their nest...

Glossary

aerial view
An aerial view is a view looking down on the ground from above.

carbon emissions
Carbon emissions are gases containing carbon that are sent into the air when we burn fossil fuels such as coal, oil and gas.

climate
Climate is the kind of weather an area usually has. For example, the climate of a tropical rainforest is hot and wet all year round.

double-glazing
Double-glazing is when two panes of glass are fitted in a window frame to prevent heat from escaping.

eco-home
An eco-home is a home designed to be friendly to the planet. It may have solar panels to heat water and double-glazing to prevent heat loss, for example.

energy
Energy is the force that makes things move, heat up or change. Renewable energy comes from sources that can be replaced or that will never run out.

environment
Your environment is what is around where you live. Your environment might be the countryside, the seaside or a city.

fertile plain
A fertile plain is a large, flat area of land with rich soil suitable for growing crops.

flat
A flat is a home with its own front door inside a bigger building.

fossil fuels
Fossil fuels are coal, oil and natural gas. We burn them to make energy. Fossil fuels are formed from the remains of ancient plants and animals.

insulation

Insulation prevents heat escaping from homes. It can be a layer of material in the loft or foam pumped into the walls.

locality

A locality is a particular area. Your locality is the area that surrounds your home.

manufactured

Materials that are manufactured are made in a factory.

materials

Materials are what things are made of. For example, bricks, concrete and wood are all types of building materials.

new town

A new town is one that has been planned and built on an open piece of land with its own schools, shops and all the things people living there need.

nomadic

Nomadic people move from place to place grazing their animals or searching for work.

settlement

A settlement is a place where people decide to live and build permanent homes.

shelter

A shelter provides cover from the weather or protection from danger.

suburb

A suburb is an area of homes built on the edge of a town or a city.

trade

Trade is the buying and selling of goods.

traditions

Traditions are things that people have been doing for hundreds of years.

Index